WHEN I WAS YOUNG
THE SEVENTIES

NEIL THOMSON
MEETS
TARUN PATEL

FRANKLIN WATTS
LONDON • SYDNEY

Tarun Patel was born in Uganda in East Africa in 1965. He is now a British citizen and lives in London. Tarun's grandparents came from Gujerat in India and settled in Uganda when both countries were under British rule.

Uganda gained independence in 1962, and nine years later the government of Milton Obote was overthrown by Idi Amin. In 1972 Amin ordered all the Asians living in Uganda to leave. More than fifty thousand people were forced to abandon their homes and businesses. Many came to Britain to make a new life.

Tarun left Uganda with his mother when he was six and came to London. He has lived since then in north-west London where he went to school and college. Tarun is an economics graduate and now works as a financial consultant with a firm in Harrow.

Paperback edition 1993

ISBN: 0 7496 0238 4 (hardback)
ISBN: 0 7496 1390 4 (paperback)

Franklin Watts
96 Leonard Street
London EC2A 4RH

Franklin Watts Australia
14 Mars Road
Lane Cove, NSW 2066

CONTENTS

Born in Uganda

My name is Tarun Patel. I was born in Kampala in Uganda in 1965. My dad was called Chandrakant Patel. He worked as a motor engineer and his job took him all over East Africa. He died in a road accident when I was very young. I never had any brothers or sisters.

I lived with my mother and my grandmother in a house in Coronation Street in Kampala. My mum was born in Kampala, where her dad had a grocery business. He'd come originally from Gujerat in India, where we still have relatives in his village.

My mum, dad and I when I was very young.

My parents' marriage was arranged by my grandparents.

My grandma lived with us; she used to bath me outside.

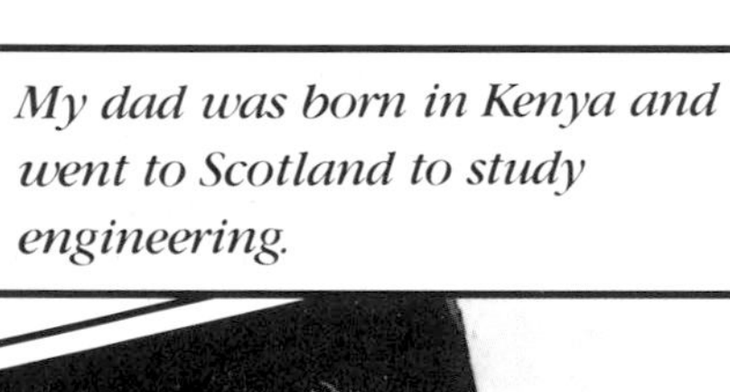

My dad was born in Kenya and went to Scotland to study engineering.

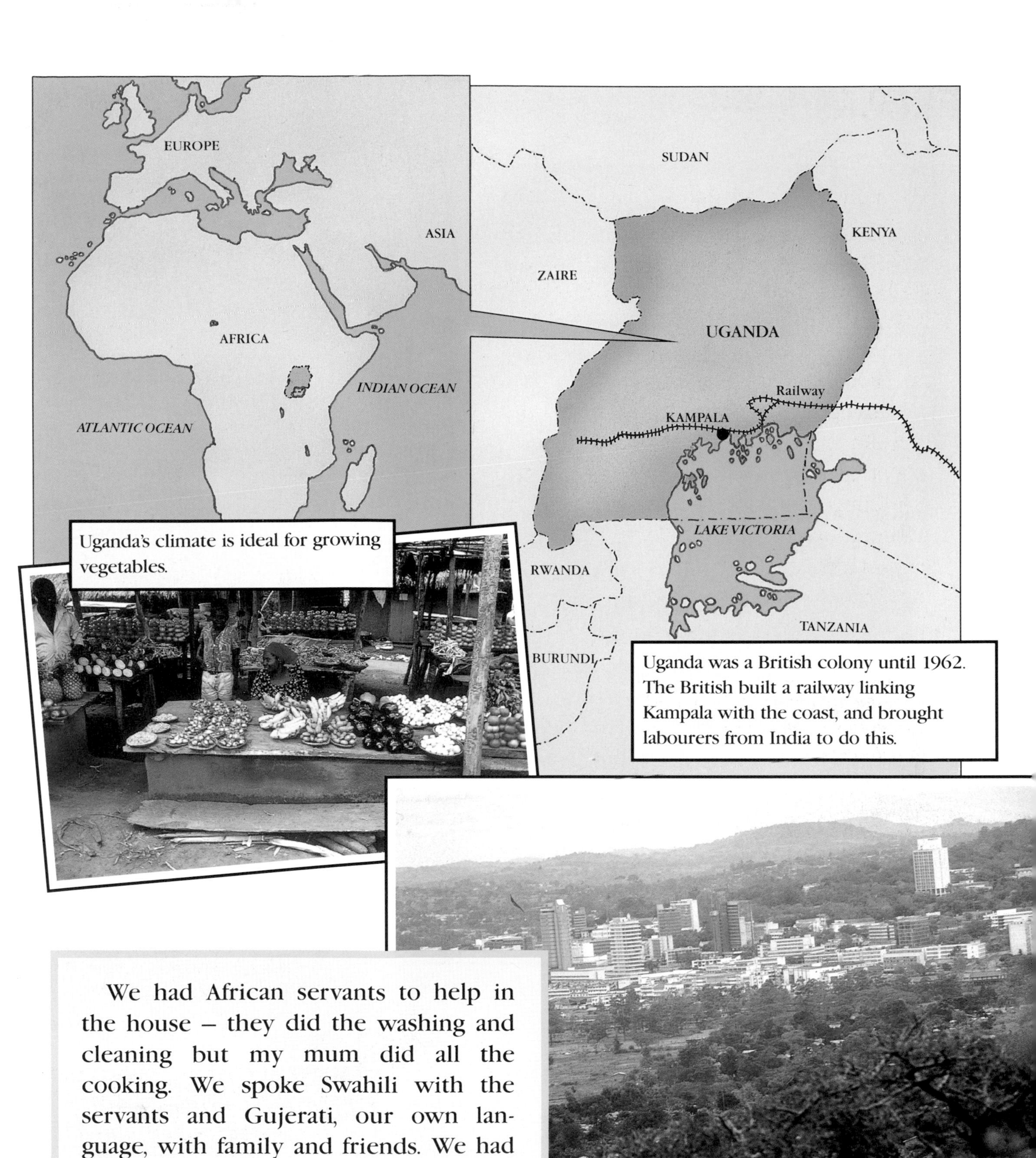

Uganda's climate is ideal for growing vegetables.

Uganda was a British colony until 1962. The British built a railway linking Kampala with the coast, and brought labourers from India to do this.

Kampala is an expanding modern city.

We had African servants to help in the house – they did the washing and cleaning but my mum did all the cooking. We spoke Swahili with the servants and Gujerati, our own language, with family and friends. We had a two-hour siesta every afternoon when it was hot. There was plenty of good food and everything was very easy.

Exodus

In Uganda most of the shops and businesses were run by Asians like us. We weren't rich but we had a comfortable life. It all changed when Idi Amin came to power and said that all the Asians would have to leave. We were given seventy-two hours to get out. Everybody was in a panic about where they were going to go.

My dad had lived in Britain and we had British passports, so my mum decided to take me and my grandma to London. As soon as we could, we got tickets and went to Entebbe airport. There were army checkpoints everywhere and the soldiers made sure you weren't taking any valuables out. The army kept a bonfire burning and people were made to throw their suitcases on it. We just gave the servants the keys to the house and the car and left, taking only the clothes we were wearing and a few pounds. We were poor when we arrived in London.

Idi Amin was an army officer who seized power in 1971.

Asian shops were closed and abandoned by their owners.

Baggage had to be left behind at Entebbe airport.

WEATHER:
Dry, sunny.
Lighting-up time:
8.19 p.m.
Details—Back Page.

46,078

Evening Standard

London: Thursday August 31 1972 6 3p

CLOSING PRICES STOP PRESS

From Mary Kenny, the only reporter to observe the airport tragedies of Uganda's departing Asians

STRIPPING OF THE BANISHED

KAMPALA, Thursday.

I STOOD at Entebbe Airport, some 22 miles from Kampala, late last night and watched Asians check in for a flight departing to London. They were a despondent, melancholy collection of people.

A man stood at the Customs barrier with a watch and 60 Ugandan shillings in his hand, shaking his head glumly. "My friend was found with an extra watch and 60 shillings. He was told to leave them here." The friend departed for London divested of any extra possessions."

I went into the Customs Hall and saw a Customs officer slowly going through every item of baggage belonging to a young Asian couple, while their two small children cried and whimpered with a child's fatigue.

The Customs officer asked me my business. I said I wanted to find out if it was true that Asians were being stripped of their property at the airport.

'Madam..it is our duty..'

"Well madam," he replied perfectly politely, "there are regulations which it is our duty to enforce. Come this way and I will show you."

He led me into a small office and pointed to a typed notice, marked with the stamp of the Collector of Customs and Excise, on the wall. This was a list of items which each departing Asian may take, namely.

- Two hundred kgs. of unaccompanied soft furnishings, such as bed sheets and blankets; all kitchenware prohibited, 20 kgs. of soft personal belongings.
- Fifty pounds per head of family foreign currency only, not one shilling of Ugandan money.
- In jewellery: one ring, one watch, two bangles, one necklace, one pair of ear-rings. Nothing to be more than 15 carat gold.

I asked the officer if everything over and above must be confiscated. "Yes," he replied. "These are the regulations; in some places we may use our discretion." He was a very reasonable man. "I am sorry about it, and I am sorry for them, but these are the regulations and we must enforce them."

The people were searched personally and he emphasised that there were two policewomen on duty to search women. I was then obliged to leave the Customs Hall, since I was not an outgoing passenger, and the customs man returned to searching the baggage of the Asian couple.

By chance, the army was not at the airport last night so things were relatively relaxed. I understand that everything is much tougher when there is a military presence; since all

Continued on Page 7

Inflation warning: Barber plays it cool

By ROBERT CARVEL

[CH]ANCELLOR Anthony [Ba]rber and his Treasury [ad]visers stuck today to [op]timistic view about [Br]itain's economic [pr]ospects.

[T]hey did so in face of the [fore]cast by the unofficial [Nat]ional Institute of Econ[omi]c and Social Research [that] there will soon be a [n] acceleration in the [rate] of inflation, calling for [] measures to counter it.

[It] was acknowledged in [Whi]tehall, however, that a great [deal] must depend on the out[come] of the tripartite discus[sion]s now going on between the [Go]vernment, the Confederation [of] British Industry and the [T]rades Union Congress.

These are aimed at restraining both prices and wages, and considerable importance is attached to the next meeting of the three sides arranged for September 14.

Unspoken thought

Nothing is officially admitted about possible changes in the direction of Government policy.

But the unspoken thought in official circles is that if this [a]ttempt by the Government [t]o stabilise the position is [u]nsuccessful then some more [f]ormalised kind of prices and [in]comes control will probably [h]ave to be devised within a few [m]onths.

As for the National Institute's [p]rediction generally — the [T]reasury view—based on its own [bit]ter experiences—is that all [e]conomic forecasting is [haz]ardous and who is to say [th]at anybody is bound to be [rig]ht?

Inflation, the killer drug of Britain, by David Malbert: Page 35

[Bo]nd and shares hit Page 34

Evening Standard

JOAN BAKEWELL, TV interviewer and former star of BBC-2's Late Night Line-up, has filed a divorce petition against her husband Michael Bakewell.

It appears in the undefended list to be heard in London. Joan, 38, names a woman called Morris.

The Bakewells met at Cambridge, where Joan was reading economics. They married in 1954. There are two children, aged 13 and eight.

Michael was head of BBC plays from 1964 to 1966.

Joan left Late Night Line Up at the end of July. She is now doing a Man Alive series called Times Remembered.

She is also doing 12 interviews for the religious department of the BBC under the title The Open Persuaders.

Some Asian families went to Canada, others to Kenya, and some to India.

A new life in England

When we first arrived in England we went straight to my uncle's house in Harrow. He worked shifts at the Kodak factory. I was the youngest in the house. With my aunts, uncles and us there were nine people altogether in a three-bedroomed house.

Our first winter here I felt very cold, I always had to have an extra jumper on. It was the first time I'd ever seen snow. My uncle woke me up to see it at about two o'clock in the morning. It was a complete surprise.

We had to move when my uncle bought a newsagent's shop in Hoddesdon and the house was sold. It was difficult to find anywhere to live then as lots of people wouldn't let rooms to Asians. Mum found a house in Wembley and sublet some of the rooms to another Gujerati family to help pay the rent.

My second winter in England

In the early 1970s there were few cars in Tarun's street.

The same street today.

We couldn't speak English when we first arrived in London. To begin with, we watched a lot of TV. We liked 'Magic Roundabout'; we learnt quite a bit of English from that. My grandma never learnt English so we always spoke Gujerati with her. She lives in India now.

An Asian friend helped Mum get a job at the local Post Office; it was the first job she'd had in her life. She worked there for fourteen years.

Programmes for 8 November

BBC1

Wednesday tv

7.30 am Colour
USA Election Special

1.0 Colour
Pebble Mill at One

4.55 Colour
The Aeronauts

Magic Roundabout
Created by SERGE DANOT
English version written and told by ERIC THOMPSON

12.30 pm Colour
Nai Zindagi

4.40 Colour
Jackanory

THE MAGIC ROUNDABOUT abc & COUNTING BOOK

DEAN

HUMBER
HILLMAN
SUNBEAM

Wembley  Observer

PUBLISHED TUESDAY AND FRIDAY

Friday, September 1, 1972

Price 4p

'Asian community in Wembley has proved exemplary in conduct'

NO COUNCIL HOUSES FOR THE REFUGEES

AS the first group of Asian refugees from Uganda prepares to come to Wembley, a statement has come from Brent Council that no local family will be put back on the housing waiting list because of the new arrivals.

Local leaders of the established Asian community in Wembley have promised to do all they can to see that no undue strain is placed on the borough's welfare services when the immigrants arrive.

'Will move on'

DETERMINED TO MAINTAIN STANDARDS

'Obviously these people have to go somewhere'

Nobody there to be rescued

Tarun's mother, Ushaben, worked here.

Starting school

My mum went along to the nearest school to see if I could start there. The head said, "Your son will be the first Indian child in the school. I'll look after him". Mum started crying when the teacher was nice to her. She hardly spoke any English then although she could understand quite a bit. I couldn't speak English either so I wasn't any help at all.

It was all a bit of a shock to me, the whole thing was completely new. I couldn't understand the teacher, and the other kids in the class all had different coloured skin from me. It felt very strange. I'd been too young to go to school in Uganda so Mum felt lonely to begin with and sat outside the classroom all morning waiting for me to come out.

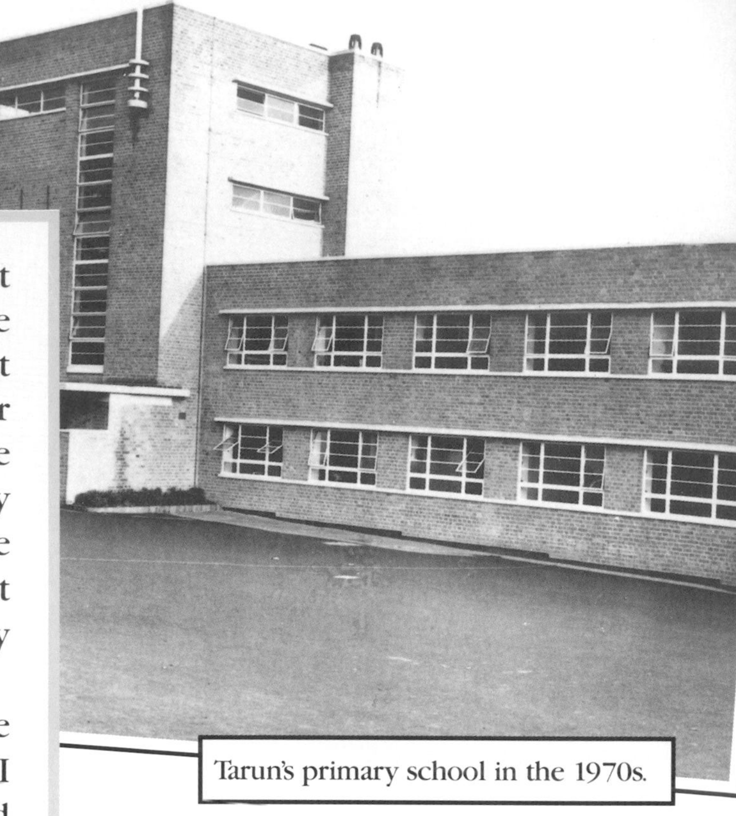

Tarun's primary school in the 1970s.

Desks from Tarun's old classroom.

Me on my friend's bike. I hadn't learnt how to ride it then.

I was pretty quiet at first, especially in breaktime, but then I started playing football and got quite excited. We had a light plastic ball so we couldn't break the windows. The girls and boys were kept separated in the playground by a line of teachers.

After school I'd go to my friend's house; we were the only two Asian boys in the class in my first year. His mum used to look after us until mine came to pick me up after she'd finished work. On Saturday there was no school, so no babysitting. I'd have to go to the Post Office with my mum. She worked and I sat by the counter. If I sat quietly until one o'clock, when she finished, we'd go to the newsagent and I'd get a chocolate.

Tarun's primary school today.

I'd buy a Curly Wurly or a Milky Way.

Playtime

I joined the Cubs early on. I belonged to the third Wembley troop. We met on Mondays and I always rushed home afterwards to watch "The Waltons" on telly. I couldn't wait for Arkala to say "Cubs, dismiss!" so that I could get back in time.

We had a craze for marbles; they came pretty high up the list for pocket money. I bought mine from the corner shop. It's run by Asians now but it wasn't then. I had over a thousand marbles; during break it was big business swapping and winning them.

When the conker season came, the marbles got packed away. There were special shaped conkers called the cheese and the double cheese, that was one with two flat edges. I got Mum to put them in the oven or the freezer to make them hard.

I always got pocket money from both my mum and my grandma, who lived with us. I did pretty well – better than most of my friends, I think. I had to account for every penny.

I saved a little in my Post Office piggy bank – Mum kept the key.

The Cubs met near our house.

MBLEY & SUDBURY DISTRICT SCOUT COUNCIL

The Scout Association

Certificate

to

TARAN PATEL of the 3RD WEMBLEY Pack

on gaining Maximum Points (15) PLAIN BISCUITS Class

1975 Cub Scout Handicraft Competition.

22.11.1975.

District Commissioner.

Once I read English well I became really keen on comics, I had a big collection. I'd run down to the newsagent's with my pocket money after school and read the comics right there. I couldn't wait till I got home. Some of my friends collected stamps but I never did. That was funny, really, since it might have been easy with my mum working in the Post Office.

At school we collected football stickers, the favourites were Tottenham Hotspur. There was a newsagent's nearby which sold stickers but they only let two kids in at a time so we used to boycott it. That shop's gone now, it's a tandoori chicken place.

We went shopping for clothes to M&S on Wembley High Road. If we wanted special foods we had to go to Popat Stores on Ealing Road. That was the only Asian food store around then, now almost the whole road is Asian.

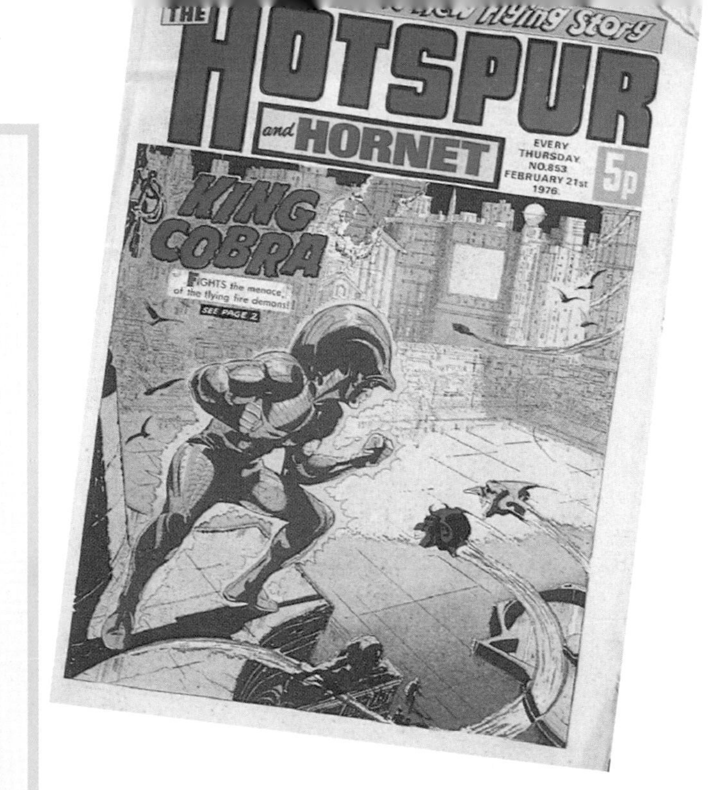

Today there are many successful Asian businesses in Wembley.

Ealing Road in the 1970s.

Secondary school

A few more Asian kids came to my primary school in my second year. Some of our neighbours were Asian and by my fourth year at that school there were quite a lot. When I went to secondary school, it was completely mixed.

We were given a New Testament at school, whatever our religion. Every morning we had a Christian assembly. You didn't have to sing the hymns if you were Asian, but I enjoyed it. Everybody said the prayers and you had to say them properly even if you didn't understand the words.

No one ever took the mickey out of me for being Asian. I was lucky, though, lots of Asian kids did suffer. Later on I was quite good at sports, and I think that helped me get accepted.

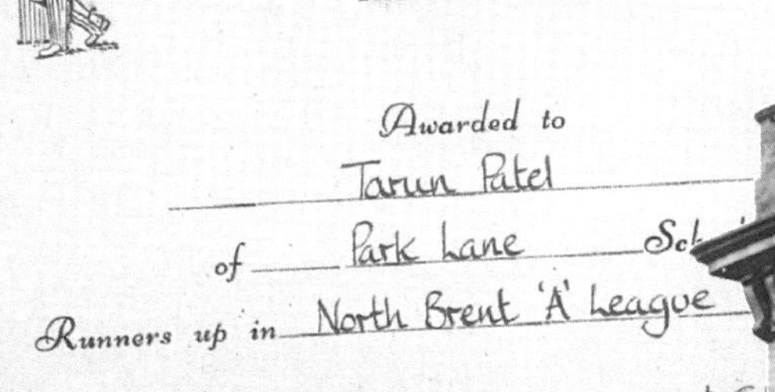

BRENT SCHOOLS' CRICKET ASSOCIATION

Awarded to Tarun Patel

of Park Lane Sc…

Runners up in North Brent 'A' League

July 1976

The main buildings of Alperton High School.

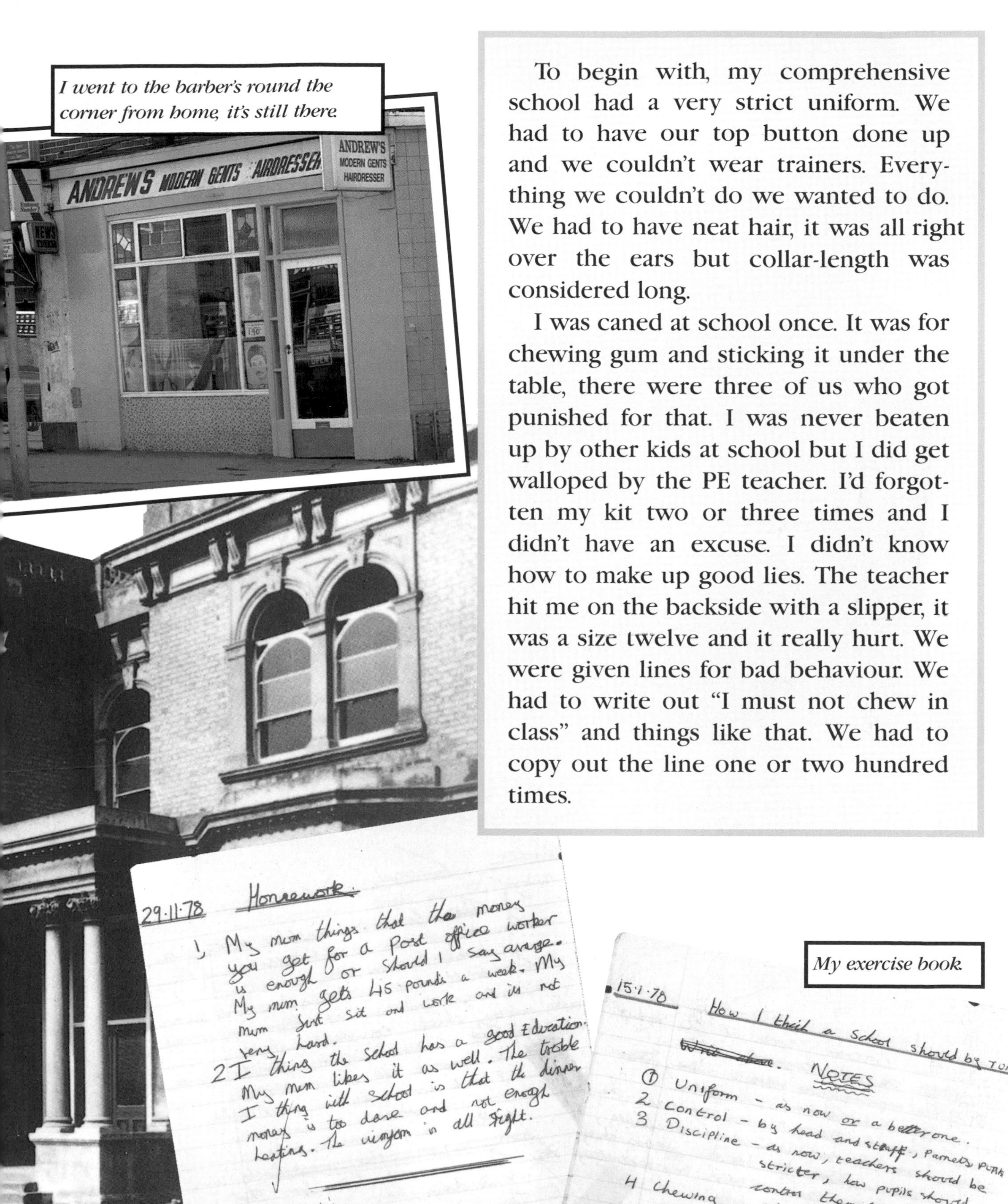

I went to the barber's round the corner from home, it's still there.

To begin with, my comprehensive school had a very strict uniform. We had to have our top button done up and we couldn't wear trainers. Everything we couldn't do we wanted to do. We had to have neat hair, it was all right over the ears but collar-length was considered long.

I was caned at school once. It was for chewing gum and sticking it under the table, there were three of us who got punished for that. I was never beaten up by other kids at school but I did get walloped by the PE teacher. I'd forgotten my kit two or three times and I didn't have an excuse. I didn't know how to make up good lies. The teacher hit me on the backside with a slipper, it was a size twelve and it really hurt. We were given lines for bad behaviour. We had to write out "I must not chew in class" and things like that. We had to copy out the line one or two hundred times.

My exercise book.

I wasn't in any of the gangs at school. There were always the tough guys and inter-school fights, but I didn't get involved. When I was fourteen the skinhead craze started. The skinheads had really short haircuts and often had tattoos. They wore Doc Marten boots, but they had to keep their trousers over the tops of their boots in school. They wrote "Skins" in all the books and called all the Asian kids "Paki". The skinheads all left the school before the sixth form so they didn't bother us for long.

Then there were the Teddy boys with Elvis haircuts and sharp-toed shoes, they never sat near the skinheads. When the teachers had to find kids to be prefects there wasn't much choice, once they'd excluded the Skins and the Teds, so I got to be a prefect.

Me in my school sweater, aged fourteen.

Groups like Showaddywaddy made Teddy boy styles fashionable.

Harold Wilson resigned as Prime Minister in 1976.

Margaret Thatcher was the first woman Prime Minister in Britain.

The chip shop near Tarun's school.

There weren't many punks at my school.

At school the teachers talked a bit about what was happening in the news. When Harold Wilson was Prime Minister some of us used to imitate him. We said, "The man with the pipe is our leader". During the General Election in 1979 we were asked what we would do if we were Prime Minister. I said, "Take all the money from the rich and give it to the poor".

I went down to the polling booth with my mum when she went to vote. I stayed up till three in the morning to see the results on TV. Then we got up early to watch the news with Thatcher getting in.

There were quite a few strikes while I was at school but we never had any days off. When the dinner ladies went on strike we all went out for lunch, and the chip shop down the road made a lot of money. We went to the park, ate chips, and made fun of the girls.

Entertainment

I liked most pop music and I loved "Top of the Pops". I watched it every week. My favourites were Gary Glitter and the Bay City Rollers. I had posters of them up in my room. I liked the Boomtown Rats too, they had a good beat. My schoolfriends went to pop concerts but I never did. I'd have liked to go but my mum didn't want me to, she'd have worried about it. I always had to tell her where I was going and what time I'd be back. I didn't much like Indian music then but I used to play the tabla. I've still got my old set. I liked playing that, it was all rhythm.

My friend played acoustic guitar. He was Spanish, and he was pretty good. Whatever he did I always wanted to do but I never learnt to play much, apart from the tune from the film "The Good, the Bad and the Ugly". We loved westerns.

IN I ASKED READERS
"POP POLL" ELECTION.

The response was tremendous and below you will see the result.

Included in the list are the pop stars who received the most votes, and it should remembered that the pop scene is ever changing and the most popular stars of last May not necessarily the most popular today.

Take David Essex for example. When we ran the poll he was in America and had been out of the limelight while making a film. It could be that if I ran the poll today, he would be amongst the leaders.

he result, and a big thank you to who took the trouble to write in.

4. ...ust
5. Osmonds (including Donny, Jimmy and Marie)
5. Suzi Quatro
6. Mud
7. Sweet
8. David Bowie
9. David Cassidy
10. Olivia Newton John
11. Bay City Rollers
12. Wizzard
Barry Blue

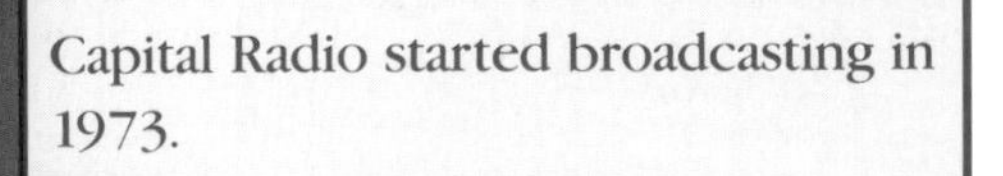

Capital Radio started broadcasting in 1973.

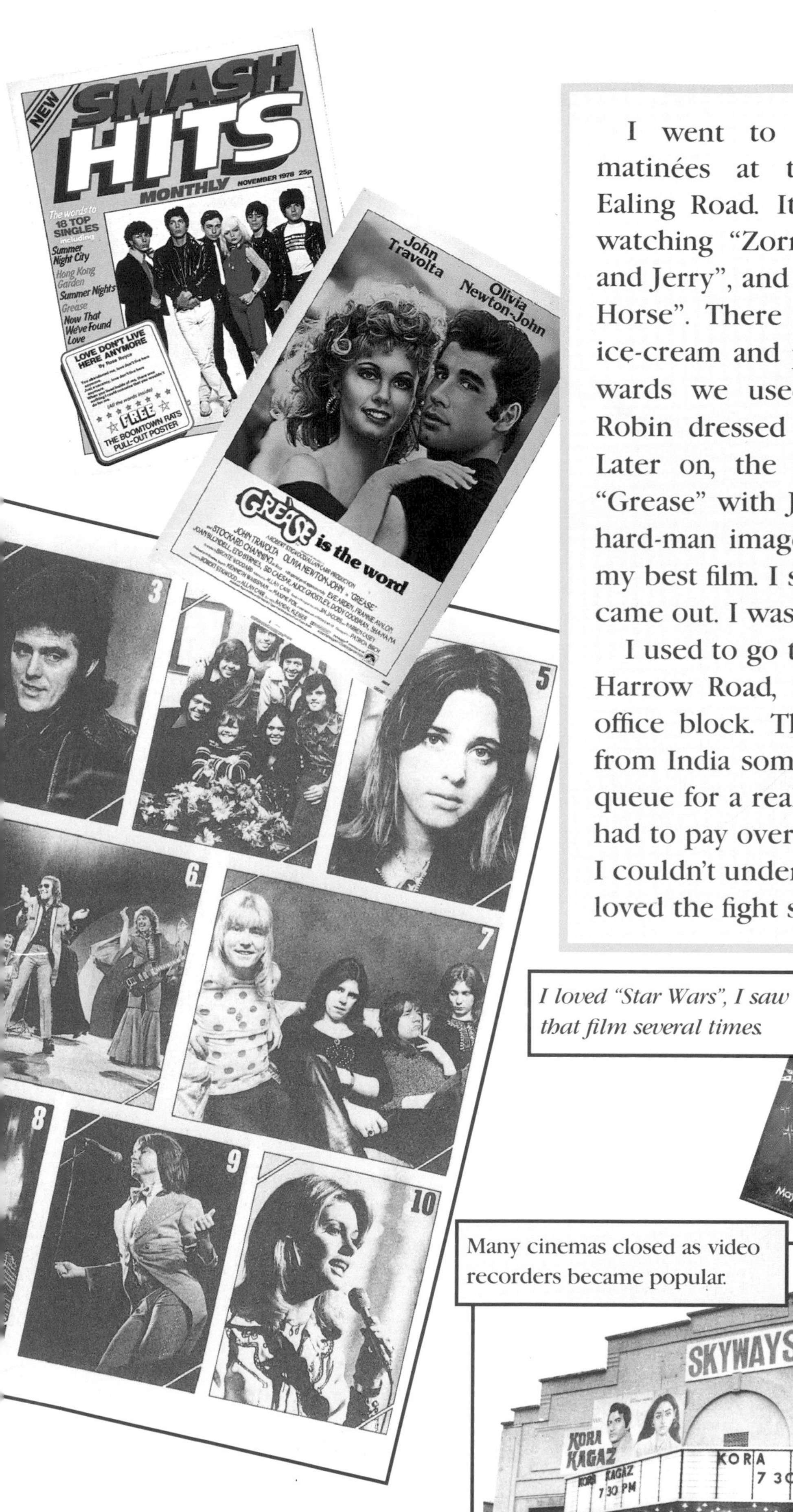

I went to the Saturday morning matinées at the Odeon cinema in Ealing Road. It was packed with kids watching “Zorro”, cartoons like “Tom and Jerry”, and “Champion, the Wonder Horse”. There was always a break for ice-cream and popcorn. At home afterwards we used to play Batman and Robin dressed up in my mum’s cape. Later on, the film I really liked was “Grease” with John Travolta, I liked his hard-man image and the music. It was my best film. I saw it twice when it first came out. I was thirteen then.

I used to go to the Liberty cinema on Harrow Road, that’s gone now, it’s an office block. They showed Hindi films from India sometimes. There’d be a big queue for a really popular film, and you had to pay over the odds to get a ticket. I couldn’t understand the dialogue but I loved the fight scenes and the songs.

I loved “Star Wars”, I saw that film several times.

Many cinemas closed as video recorders became popular.

Sports

When I was eleven we moved house to quite near Wembley Stadium. It was really good fun on Cup Final days. A couple of my friends would come round and we'd stand at the front of the house and watch the coaches going by. We waved at the fans of the team we supported and shouted "Boo" at the others. We got away with that because we were too small then for any trouble.

I collected cricketers' autographs. I managed to get nearly all the great ones. I used to hang around outside the ground after a match and wait for them to come out. I was a keen player until I broke my thumb and my collar bone while I was batting in the nets against a demon bowler.

EMPIRE STADIUM WEMBLEY
Assoc. Football
ENGLAND v ITALY
16/11/77

THE EMPIRE STADIUM, WEMBLEY
Association Football
INTERNATIONAL MATCH
(World Cup Qualifying)
No ticket genuine unless it carries a Lion's Head watermark below
ENGLAND
VERSUS
ITALY
WED. NOV. 16, 1977
TURNSTILES C
KICK-OFF 7.45 p.m.
YOU ARE ADVISED TO TAKE UP YOUR POSITION BY 7.15 p.m.
ENTRANCE 10
EAST UPPER STANDING ENCLOSURE
CHAIRMAN: WEMBLEY STADIUM LTD
342
STANDING
£2.50
O BE RETAINED
SEE PLAN AND CONDITIONS ON BACK

I went to the match at Wembley. England won.

I've still got my old bat and pads.

ENGLAND
Possible contenders

IAN BOTHAM. Somerset. 23. Right-arm medium bowler and right-hand bat. 23 wickets, and 291 runs in winter Tests.

GEOFF BOYCOTT. Yorkshire. 38. Right-hand opening batsman. Played in 80 Tests and has scored over a hundred centuries.

MIKE BREARLEY. Middlese 36. Right-hand batsman. Has l England in 19 tests, winning drawing 5 and losing one.

PHIL EDMONDS. Middlesex. 28. Left-arm spinner and right-hand batsman. Made Test debut v Australia in 1975.

JOHN EMBUREY. Middlesex. 26. Off-spin bowler. Took 16 wickets, av. 19.13 v Australia in winter.

MIKE GATTING. Middlesex. 21. Right-hand batsman, right-arm medium pace bowler and excellent fielder.

GRAHAM GOOCH. Essex. 25. All-rounder who scored 246 runs, av. 22.36 in last winter's series, with a top score of 74.

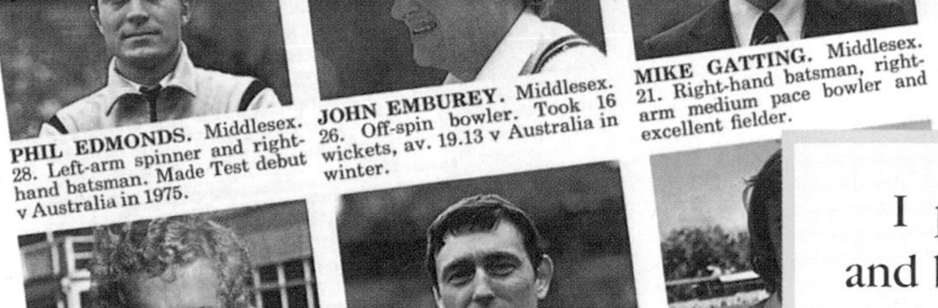

DAVID GOWER. Leicestershire. 22. Left-hand bat. Topped Test averages in Australia, scoring 420 runs, av. 42.

MIKE HENDRICK. Derbyshire. 30. Right-arm fast-medium bowler. Topped winter tour averages with 28 wickets, av. 14.25.

JOHN LEV arm fast c right-hand wickets in

medium nd first-rate slip d in 41 Tests.

I supported the Campaign for Nuclear Disarmament.

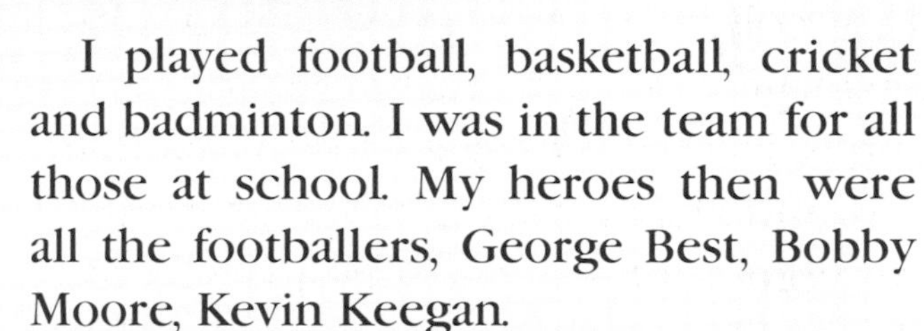

I played football, basketball, cricket and badminton. I was in the team for all those at school. My heroes then were all the footballers, George Best, Bobby Moore, Kevin Keegan.

I played darts with my friends and a lot of ping-pong. I had my own bat and used to play down at the community centre.

I had to have a skateboard when the craze first started. It cost £10, that was a lot of money then. I had the pads and the whole kit and used to practise on the street.

I always dreaded going to swimming classes. In Uganda there weren't any pools and it was far from the sea so I'd never learnt to swim there. I did get my 10-metre certificate but then I gave it up. I hated cross-country running, I used to take a short cut and then wait for a few people to come by. Then I'd run the last bit and look whacked so the teachers wouldn't know I'd cheated.

Things to buy

My first birthday in England. I always got a big present.

We never had much money when I was young. Mum didn't earn much at her Post Office job and prices kept going up all the time. We never celebrated Christmas much at home, but Mum always asked me what I wanted for my birthday. One year digital watches had just come out and that was what I badly wanted, even though I already had an ordinary watch. I got one of those Texas Instruments ones with a little light.

My uncle used to buy me the more expensive presents – he got me a bike for my tenth birthday. It was a "Chopper", that was the in-thing then. I had a Casio calculator, it was thick and the buttons made a noise when you pressed them. We weren't allowed calculators in class till I was fifteen. We had to use slide rules and really had to know our times tables.

I had a Sony Walkman pretty soon after they came out. I never had a ghetto blaster, though lots of other kids did.

I learnt to use a slide rule to do calculations.

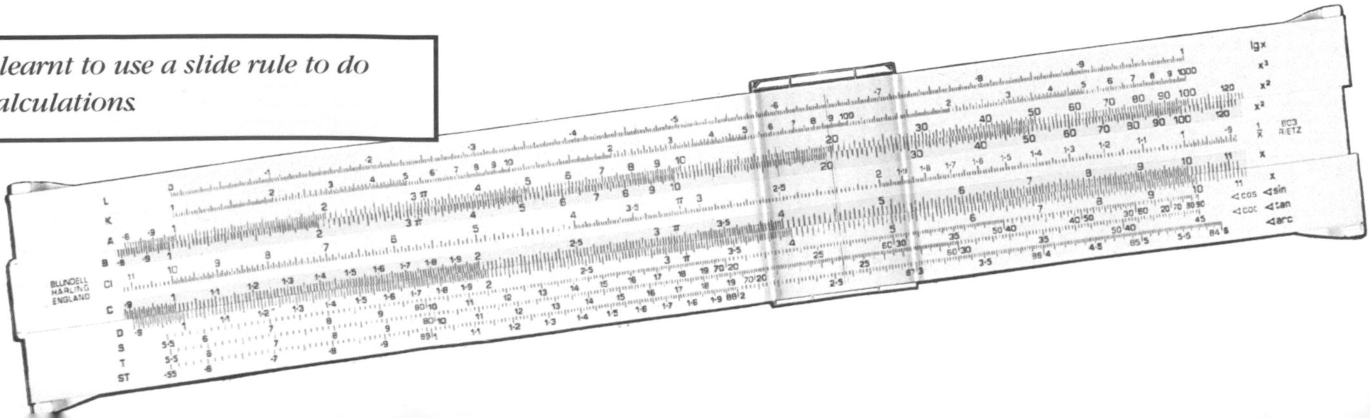

If your bike had three gears you were doing really well.
THE HOT ONE
Ride the bike with burn-up potentia
Straddle the hottest number Raleigh have
ever produced.
Chopper. A machine inspired by the
screaming rubber and roaring fantails of
the dragster racing slick.
Chopper, designed on lean, taut, tear
away-and-love-it lines. For guys and gals
who want a bike built for action. With th
lid off!
You've never known anything like
Chopper. It took the U.S.A. by storm.
With its high-rise "apchanger" handleba
Coil-spring shock absorbers. Drag-style
saddle. Chrome roll bar. And snap-action
shift that flashes change of pace instantly
from the crossbar.
Wow your pals on Chopper. Turn
heads as you rip away. Own a machine
with muscle to spare.
Chopper. The hot one!
CHOPPER
CHOPPER
10:10
Quartz
10:10
Quartz
LCD
CASIO fx-29
SCIENTIFIC CALCULATOR
You're never too old
We didn't have a car. My mum never learnt to drive and, anyway, I don't think we could have afforded one.

Weekends

On Sundays we always went to our temple in Islington. The temple is a very special place for us. We're members of a Hindu sect, followers of the Swami Narayan movement. When I was older the temple moved to a converted warehouse near where we lived. By that time the Saturday matinées had stopped at the cinema and we had religious school at the temple.

Our guru came from India to open the new temple. He arrived by helicopter on my school playing-field and then toured the area on an elephant in pouring rain. All the kids followed him for about five hours. Our guru is a religious teacher, he shows you how you can become a better person.

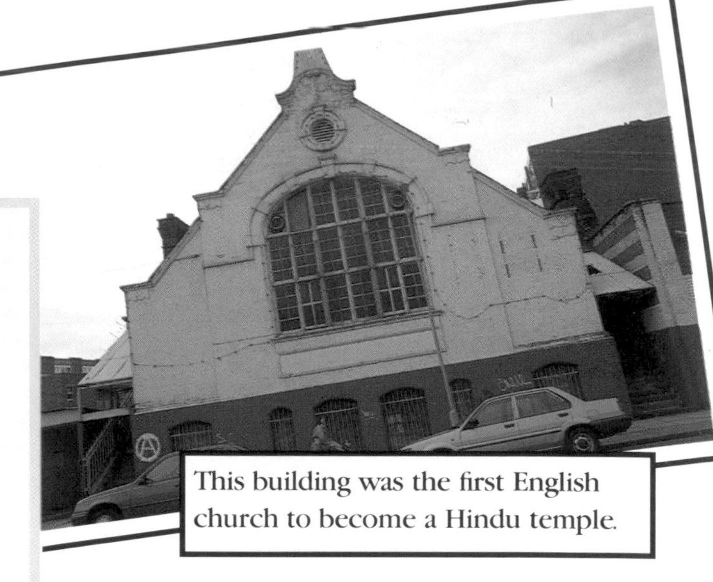

This building was the first English church to become a Hindu temple.

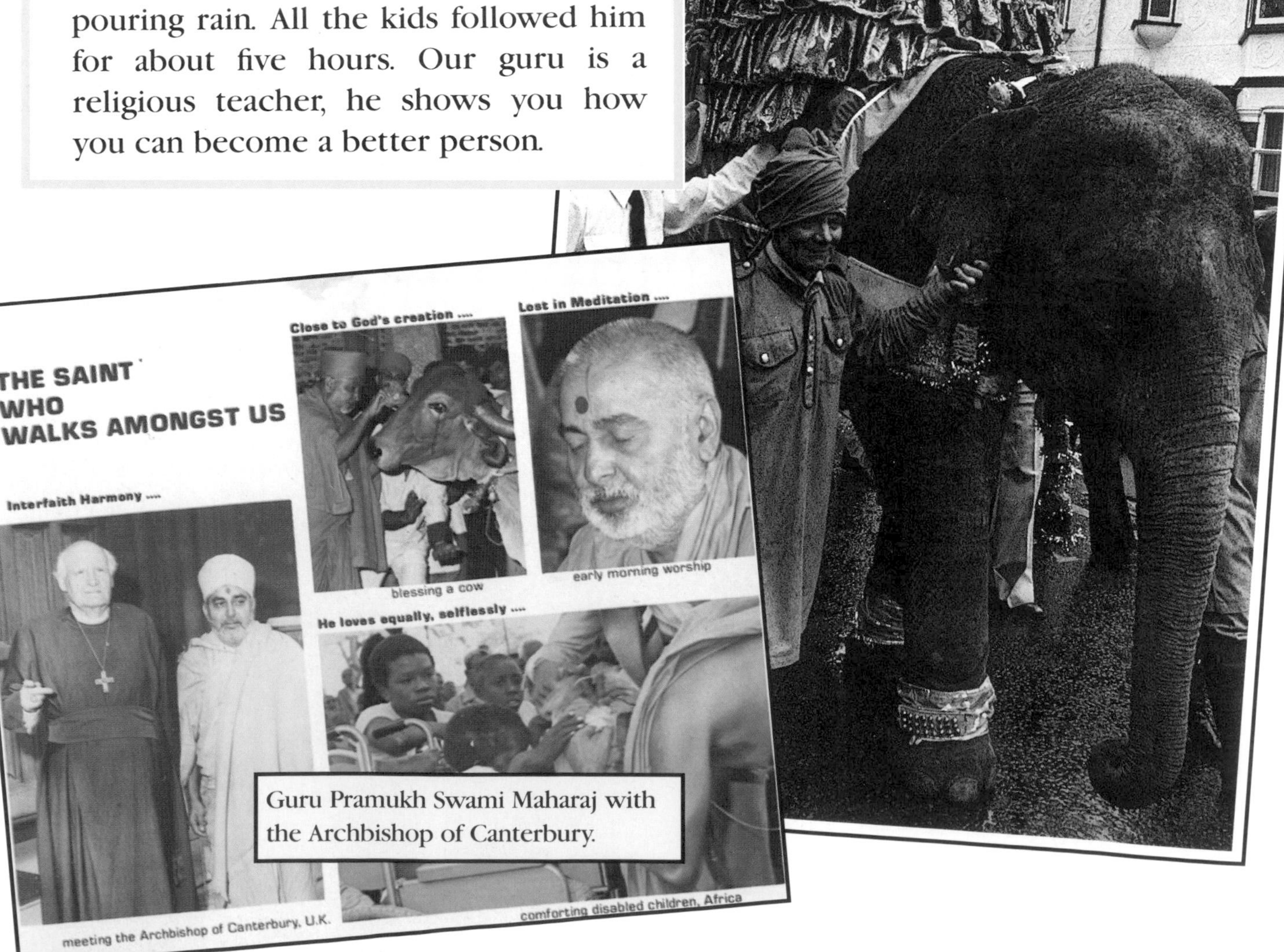

Guru Pramukh Swami Maharaj with the Archbishop of Canterbury.

Me in the front row at a wedding.

McDonalds opened in Wembley in the 1970s.

Like most Hindus we always ate vegetarian food at home, but my mum said I should eat meat when I was out if there wasn't any choice. I quite liked sausages and burgers so it was a great thing when McDonalds opened in Wembley. I stopped eating meat after I met our guru. He said I should become a vegetarian and that I shouldn't smoke or drink if I wanted to be a good Hindu.

We often went to family weddings at the weekends. There'd be a big party, it would go on a long time with lots of food and music. Some of my cousins had arranged marriages. Mostly, though, if a boy wanted to marry a girl he'd go to an older brother or uncle and say, "I want to marry so and so, please pass a message to her parents". If all the parents agreed, the wedding would go ahead. My mum might introduce me to a suitable girl when the time comes for me to marry and I certainly wouldn't marry anyone she didn't approve of.

I learnt a lot of Hindu stories from Indian comics.

Leaving school

I was a very keen squash player at school. My coach was the British Airways champion and he encouraged me to become a pro. He even went as far as writing to my mother to say I should make a career of it. But what I really wanted to do was to get into business.

Economics really interested me but unfortunately I wasn't any good at the exams. After I got an unclassified in my CSE, the careers adviser said, "Don't even try for economics or accountancy, go for sociology or psychology". But I got an interview at Ealing College and begged for a place even though my grades were poor. I was lucky to get in.

I finished up with a BA Honours in economics. Now I work as a business adviser, finding money for new projects. I'd really like to go into hotel development here and in Europe, that's my ambition at the moment.

ALPERTON HIGH SCHOOL
REPORT

Autumn Term, 1979

Name PATEL, Tarun Form 4H

SUBJECT	YEAR FORM etc.	GRADE or %	EFFORT	
Religious Education	Form	C	C	Tarun m...
English Language	CSE	C	C	Tarun n... at home... needs ca...
English Literature		C	C	Tarun ha...
Mathematics	O/C.S.E	C+	B	class w... please...
Geography	E1	D+	C+	Tarun t... but can... talkative... the pro...
Biology	4PH	D	C	Tarun... work... always...
Physics	E2	C	C	Tarun... makes... unsur... work
T.D	4D2	C	D	Tarun... but... any...
Computer Studies	O/CSE	D	C	A disappointing... spent less time talking in lessons... make far greater progress
P.E	4HJ	C	B	Taren has continued to prod...
Careers	H	-	B+	Satisfactory performance... well in class.

A = EXCELLENT B = VERY GOOD C = AVERAGE

In the news

These are some of the important events which happened during Tarun's childhood.

1970 In Britain, eighteen-year-olds were able to vote for the first time. Labour lost the election and Edward Heath became Prime Minister.

1972 The miners' strike forced the government to introduce the three-day working week in order to save stocks of coal.

1973 Attacks on Israel by Egypt and Syria started the October War in the Middle East. Arab oil producers raised prices by 70% to put pressure on the USA to act against Israel.

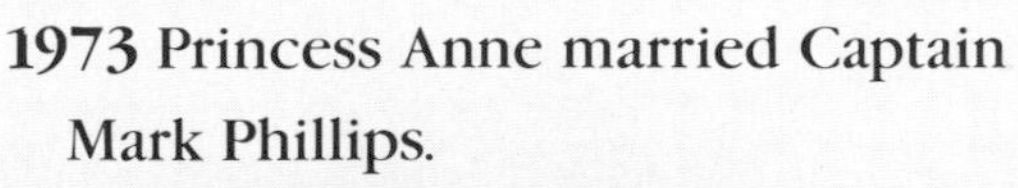

1973 Princess Anne married Captain Mark Phillips.

1974 President Nixon resigned in Washington. Turkey invaded Cyprus and many Greek Cypriot refugees came to Britain.

1975 The American forces finally withdrew from South Vietnam.

1976 Concorde started passenger flights. Chairman Mao Tse-Tung, the Chinese leader, died.

1977 In 1977 there were street parties throughout Great Britain to celebrate the Queen's Silver Jubilee.

1978 The wrecked oil tanker *Amoco Cadiz* caused a pollution disaster in the English Channel.

1979 The Shah of Iran was overthrown and Ayatollah Khomeini returned from exile in Paris to take power.

Things to do

Make a 1970s scrapbook

Many of your relatives or neighbours will have memories of the 1970s. Their experiences may have been very different from those of Tarun Patel. Show them this book and ask them how their life in the 1970s compared.

If you have a cassette recorder you could tape their memories. Before you visit people, make a list of the things you want to talk about – for example, music, clothes, films, school, sports. Some people may have kept photos of the period as well as magazines or records. Ask if you can look at them.

Go to your local library. Ask to see any newspapers from the 1970s. Look at books about entertainment and fashion. Compare how things looked in the 1970s with how they look now. Your library may have a local studies section. If so, ask the librarian if they have any photographs of your area from the 1970s. Compare the houses and the shops then with what there is today. Walk around your area to see what shops and businesses might have started.

Look at adverts in old magazines, and compare the prices then with how much things cost now.

Use what you find out to make a scrapbook about the 1970s.

Reading list: here is a list of other books to read on the 1970s.

Decades: The Seventies
Michael Garrett (Wayland)

Finding out about life in Britain in the 1970s
Pamela Harper (Batsford)

Growing up in the 1970s
Nance Lui Fyson (Batsford)

History of the Modern World: The Seventies
John Edwards (Macdonald Educational)

Picture History of the Twentieth Century: 1970s
Tim Healey (Franklin Watts)

Portrait of a Decade: The 1970s
Elizabeth Campling (Batsford)

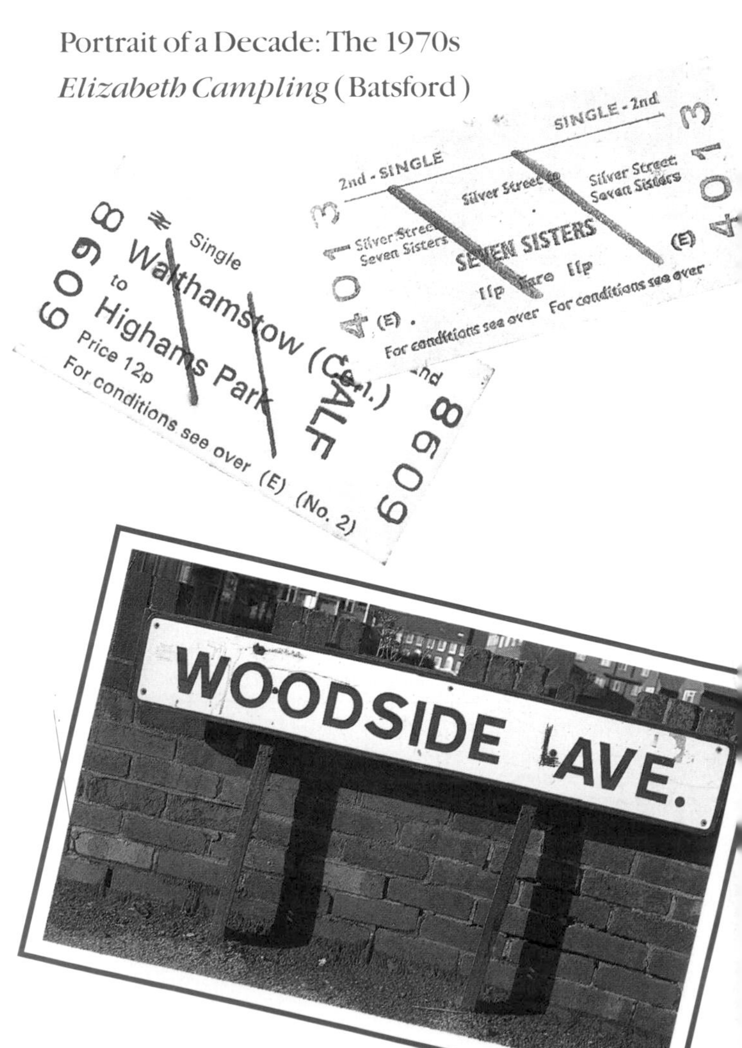

ONCE IN A LIFETIME •

A ROYAL JUBILEE • STOP

Get Radio Rentals Colour for the Jubilee weekend

On Tuesday, 7th June, the Queen delivers her historic Jubilee Broadcast to the Commonwealth.

And you could be watching in full colour on a good as new 19" tube Radio Rentals set from only £7·20 down (one month's advance rental). With reliable Radio Rentals service behind you all the way.

You also get the Radio Rentals money-back promise – all your money back if you're not completely satisfied within one month of signing.

22" and 25" tube models also available.

Immediate delivery from your local Radio Rentals branch.

Index

Series design: David Bennett
Design: Mel Raymond
Editor: Jenny Wood

Picture research: Sarah Ridley
Printed in Belgium

Acknowledgements

The author and publisher would like to thank Tarun Patel without whom this book would not have been possible. Thanks also to the Swaminarayan Temple, London.

Photography: Neil Thomson

Additional pictures: courtesy of Argos 23c; courtesy of Capital Radio 18b; Design Museum 19tl, 22c; Format/Raisa Page 16c, 17bl; John Frost Newspaper Service endpapers; Greater London Record Office/Grange Museum, London 10t, 14/15b; Harrow and Wembley Observer Series 24br; courtesy of McDonalds 25tr; National Film Archive/Lucasfilms 19bc; National Film Archive/Paramount 19tr; Newslink Africa 5c, 5b, 6c, 6b, 7c; Robert Opie 11br; Popperfoto 6t, 17tl, 17tr, 27(all), 28(all), 29(all); courtesy of Raleigh Industries 23t; Wembley History Society/Grange Museum, London 8c, 13b 19br.

The publishers have endeavoured to discover the copyright holders of material reproduced in this book. However, if anyone can give any further information, please let us know.

A CIP Catalogue record for this book is available from the British Library.